second childhood

jack jones

Celticfrog Publishing

Clearwater, BC

CELTICFROG PUBLISHING

At 93, Jack views the collection as a tribute to his mentor and friend, the late Anne Marriott, his teachers in Whitchurch, Shropshire, and a happy English childhood in spite of the Depression and World War 2.

Thanks to publisher Alex McGilvery of Celticfrog Publishing for rediscovering Rina Piccolo whose art matches the poet's imagination.

This pencil portrait of the 1980 version of the Poet Laureate is by Gine Rose.

The late composer, Art Lewis, also had artistic talent as his hockey illustration proves.

Table Of Contents

My dog doesn't have a pedigree,
a fancy name, a filigree collar,
a blue ribbon, a championship
cup. No ... All my dog's got is
ME!

Cats caterwaul
They stalk the dark
They frighten the shadows
They haunt troll corners
Creep unexpectedly
Miaoul so dejectedly
Have appendectomies
In the night

Bags —
    I like the possibilities of them,
        their secrets;
    brown, they must be brown,
        top-openable,
        bottom-drop-outable
            bags.
    Who has never received
        a wriggling, dumpy,
        alive and worrying,
            brown paper bag
    and found inside a puppy?
    Or watched a cat climb in,
        inquisitive, and take
        sniffing, whiskering
        possession of its
    bag-womb coiled-up cosiness?
        Bags —
    I'm really into bags.

the kangaroo
with a low-down
down under trick
invented the
karate kick
but
when it does it
it cheats
it uses both
its hind feet
and its tail
as an extra
long rubbery leg
anyone
who takes on
a 'roo
has got to be
a fool
kangas
are best left
to big Reds
and little Joeys
unless
you want to end up
with OUCHIES
and OHIES

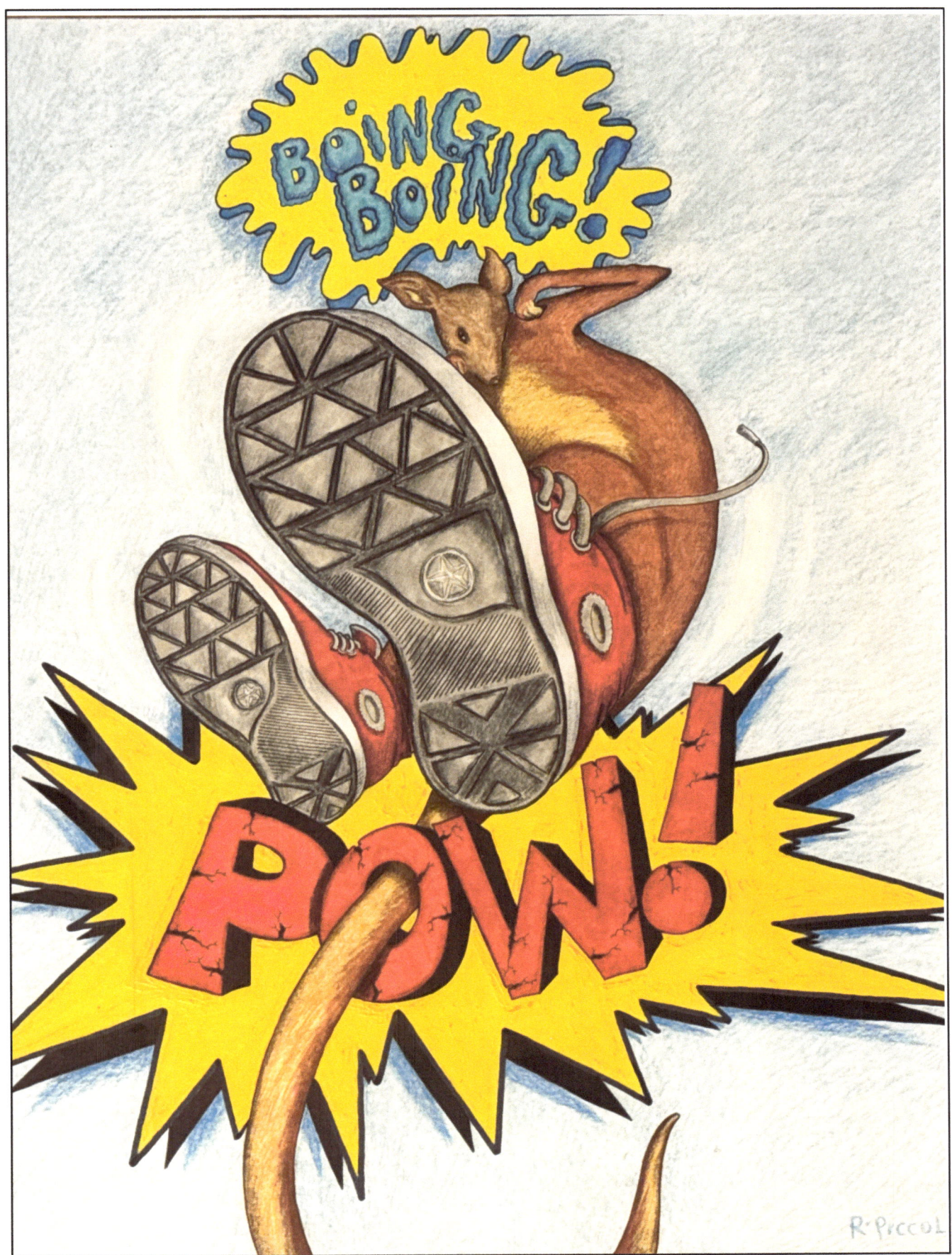

The pelican is my favorite bird...
whether it is because of that old rhyme
About its belly and its beak
And the capacity of each,
Or because of its land-borne,
Stumble-foot stand.
However, this I know --
Airborne,
It is that wonder of white
Against the sky;
Does everything to please;
Sails with a schooner's ease.

SOME FOLK THINK
bats flutter
flitter
uncontrolledly
stu-t-ter
through
s
p
a
c
e

IT'S NOT TRUE...

bats

would win prizes at electronic
if only we could see quicker air
than we thought we did displays

bats' kamikazis

aborted

twilight fox
forest shadow
perfecting your habit
of changing the season
silver paws
gold tongue
cold bletch*nose
wide shrewd eyes
and
tip of tail
all this is etched
upon my mind
the rest beautifully lost
ghosting
then
coming
as you dance
the old ways
indeterminate
as snow
fallen
on snow
more knowing than known
did I see or imagine you
fox
twilight fox

* shropshire idiom —
the black stuff you get on your
hands off a bike chain.

NIGHT WALK, McQUEEN LAKE

The crack of the crust of the snow —
Cannibal echoes.
Slow… slow… stop!
Star silence overflows.
A coyote hurls its cry
Back of du Bois.
Kids huddle;
Grown-ups wish they could!
Whiteness rises.
Pines dance about.
Hold your breath!
Far, far off a diesel locomotive purrs.

Chocolate Rabbit

Chocolate Rabbit......
       nibble his ears!
Chocolate Rabbit......
       there goes his nose!
Chocolate Rabbit......
       his mouth goes south!
Chocolate Rabbit......
       his chest goes west!
Chocolate Rabbit......
       his belly's in mine!
Chocolate Rabbit......
       his rump is divine!
Chocolate Rabbit......
       the end is nigh...

Hey! There's no tail, Mr. Cadbur-eye!

The Dinosaur Monster

The Dinosaur Monster
is green, green, green.
He comes in the night
when he can't be seen.

His nose it's a-snuffling,
he's drooling a smidgin.
His tummy's a-rumbling.
He's there in our kitchen!

"US DINOSAUR MONSTERS
JUST LOVES BIRFDAY CAKES
MORE BETTER'N PRESENTS—
THE CAKES WOT WE TAKES!"

The Dinosaur Monster
is green green **green**!
He comes in the night
when he can't be seen.

60 Below

When coldness this cold comes
it grabs the nose hairs of adults
and pulls long icicles
thin as whistles
up from roots
in the bottom lefthand
corner of their boots
- at 60 Below.

Nose hairs
confused by coldness beyond cold
cry thin and small:
"Are we upside down?
Stackletites or staglimites?
At 60 Below
a nose hair scarcely knows."

Minute fleas inhabit nose hairs
where they nibble jelly babies.
But at 60 Below
the cute ears of the ebony candy jubes
crisp to pepper particle bacony bits
causing their grown up hosts to sneeze
"GEZUNDHEITDAMMERUNG!!!"
Brains disintegrate
into dehydrated split-pea soup
- at 60 Below.

All good little Inuit children
remind Dad when into
the Arctic night he goes,
"Papa, beware of Polar bears!"
But Mom and Dad both know
what's worse at 60 Below
is to offer a grown up Inuit
licorice jujubes, or that
he should catch a glimpse
beneath the Northern Lights
of the jet black snow snuff,
inadvertently sniff the stuff...
At 60 Below
the only thing to do
is to get his mukluks
P. D. Q.
back to Tuktoyaktuk.

Summer

This is the day of
the déjà, déjà,
déjà vu butterfly.

The Lesson

Black bike
hand-painted by Dad
Shiny owner
hand-scrubbed by Mum
Sunday
I'm scared
I'll scratch
the paint
somehow spoil
the perfectness of the day
for all three of us
tied to that
weird wheeled
tube triangle
I sit upon
sweating fear pride
in equal parts
learning to ride a bike

One foot
needing the ground
the bike
banked to make it possible
feel of handgrips
the good smell of "Dunlop"
left on the hands
the ear just as pleased
when pedals in reverse
send seething
oil-gravel bearings
chasing
all the others
trapped
in the gear slot
skittering chain's
effort and force
endlessly lost
but the bike,
the leg
and the ground
remain triangulated

slow
keep it slow
I'm go-go-going
both feet pressing
no the left less
than the right
now more
press left
stirrup-less lift
right
moustache-upside-down-handlebar's smile
leather squeak seat
tense tight frame
whips warps slips
wobbles
then slides of its own free will
joy moment prolonged
solo flight
motion mastering
grim relaxed delight
"Just watch me, Mum... I'm riding a bike!"

There's a boy on the beach,
and the sea and the sand
and the sea and the sand,
                    and a boy.

And the sound of the sea,
and the feel of the sand,
and the seethe of the waves,
and the pull of the sand.

And a gull wheeling high
belongs to the sky
and the sea and the sand.

And the boy on the beach
                    stands apart;
and the sand is the sea,
and the sky up around
the inverted palm of a hand.

And the boy on the sand
                    stands,
and the land and the sky
and the sand are apart.

And the echoing roar
of the echoing roar
of the waves on the shore
takes the mind of the boy:
and the sand on the shore
is the wall of the world
with the sea at its feet.

And the sea comes and goes,
holds,
then comes, endlessly comes
and the sea is the sea
is the sea and the sand,
is one
with the sky and the sun
washing and drying the land.
And the boy on the beach
bends and writes in the sand,
    AIN'T NATURE GRAND?
    ...... high praise,
which the waves read
          and recede
          read
          and recede
          read
          and erase.

CHRISTMAS HOLIDAYS

Always the hope of snow.
In St. Alkmund's
in the choirstalls
a prayer from each angel-boy:
"Our Father,
In Your heaven of snow,
Make it come down
Like Jesus.
Amen."
And when it did
all our ugliness,
our town's Victorian industrial,
turned to Swiss celestial,
roofs ermine-corniced,
each muted road and
silent sidewalk
bedecked in beauty.

We anticipated
the muffled climb
up Terrick way
outside town,
under that
cyclists' nightmare
the "Kill-Cow,"
where Dugdale's Bank
stretched unchallenged
since when,
the longest, smoothest slope
known to man!
What scoutmaster,
apprentice carpenter,
unknown benefactor
fashioned that sled of sleds,
that paragon of toboggans
belonging to the Scouts?

Wood, all solid wood,
steel shod with runners
polished like Grandad's Boer War sword.
Generations of goggle-eyed,
breath-bereft lads
six at a time
- or was it eight? -
hurled the hill
in 100 yard dashes
to leave Jesse Owens aghast.
Before our eyes
beyond the bottom
up the slope opposite
an oak tree
we believed from Charles 1's time
(Charlie Birch was convinced of it!)
plumb centre of the run.
That oak tree was our goal
yet a threat without menace
even to our fantastic imaginings.

Prone I'd lie on the sled
like a seal - or a bullet -
the others straddling
and hanging on to
belt, pockets, scarf...Me!
And off!...the last man
bobsleigh fashion
boosting the natural volition
of the projectile
to be on its sudden way
down, down,
over and done with it.
All day till light failed
we slipped the world
and our reckless youth
beneath us,
each second stretched
as time got unhinged.

Just once
by dint of concerted willpower
on the late afternoon
ice gliss of the snow-pack
just once
we outstripped the rest
outdid every other kid
slid sledgelengths past the possible
and counted death a near-miss
as the oak stopped
back of us,
in the owl-silent night
sudden upon us
heard our own heart
or someone else's.

Here comes a candle...

There's a very small house I know, I know, I know,
With a crooked, creaking door that leans forever open.
I go in. I stand still. I look to left and right –
There's paper peeling off the wall. Not very much light
comes through the tiny window but I can see the stairs–
They're rickety and pickety. Criss–crossing is the hair
Of a hundred different spiders' webs telling me "keep out!"
But I break them all and climb right up – I know it's not fair.
At the top's a landing and a big oak balustrade
Which I can lean right over and make myself afraid
Of animals I imagine and people in the shadows.
There's witches, trolls and ogres, gnomes and skeletons;
There's slimy things and creepy things and things that hiss and groan.
But the thing of which I'm most afraid is not below downstairs –
It's not a giant, not a snake, nor an animal with hair –
It's a wooden door that stands erect at the end of the corridor.
It's as black as a coffin's inside with an eye in the middle that stares.
And behind it there's a secret that's as old as old as old.
(Dad says it isn't an eye at all, it's only a knob made of brass),
But I'm never going to touch that eye... I know I'll turn to WAX,
And whatever's inside on the other side of that terrible eye brass handle
Will light my hair and use me up as its life-like child wax candle!

Long Pants

Look, Mum! No knees!
         No scabs!
         No knocking!
But in the throat, regret!
LOST:
   A nearness to heaven.
   A next-to-godliness.
   A clean treble.

"Rosemary... that's for remembrance"

An airman went to war one day,
He went to Europe far away.
He fought and died and never came back.
His name was Jack.

A soldier went to war one day,
He went to Asia far away.
He fought and died beneath the heat.
His name was Pete.

It's at home that Rosemary blooms,
The fragrant memory lingers on.
She does not die in a single day,
She has her life to fade away:
Her brother and her lover
Both have gone.

Hockey Jingle

Hockey makes me happy!
Hockey makes me hoot!
Hockey is my game, Man!
Shoot! Shoot! Shoot!

I don't hear the crowd roar,
I don't hear my Dad.
I don't hear my Mom's yells.
Hockey's where I'm at.

Higher than an eagle.
Swifter than a hawk.
Blitzing like a Blazer.
Gee, just hear me talk!

Deke him to the right side,
Deke him to the left.
Swing across the near post,
Shoot.....it's in the net!

Hockey makes me happy!
Hockey makes me hoot!
Hockey is my game, Man!
Shoot! Shoot! Shoot!

C.P./C.N.

C.P./C.N., C.P./C.N., C.P./C.N., C.P./C.N.
Ka-am-loops! Ka-am-loops!
Canadian Pacific,
Canadian National
From Atlantic Ocean
To Ocean Pacific.
Cee-ee-Pee!
Cee-ee-en!
Everything that's easy—
Locomotive motion.
Anything hard needs
Locomotive notions.
Opening the Prairies,
Joining sea to sea,
Spiralling through mountains
Ad mare a mari.
Cee-ee-ay!
Ee-en-pee!
Canadian Atlantic??

National Pacific??
What does it mean
To the B.C. Interior?
What are they after
At Stump Lake or Barriere?
Ti-im-ber!
Ti-im-ber!
For Maritime masts that are trailing through clouds,
For B.C. H.B.'s for writing this down!
For boats and neat bungalows,
Horse floats, framed windows;
For doors, for floors, for walls, for halls—
Whatever, wherever.
Ti-im-ber!
Ka-am-loops!
C.P./C.N., C.P./C.N.
Take it away! Take it away! Take it away!
Today! Today!
Now! (Clap!)

A book shut up -
it is the flattest, silentest thing,
two no better than one.
Like that folded paper tissue sachet
from Japan
which Dad bought
from a gypsy at the fair,
a paper twist
that's all.
Bored by its ordinariness
we watched
when Dad let it drop
into a jar of water,
this paper nothing
and wondered at his "Wait and see!"

Sudden magic:
Fujiyama Mountain,
new dawn,
cherry blossom snowed-on hillsides,
carnations, blood tipping
the pinkest petals.

A book open
opens up other places, others:
we see through gypsy eyes,
live Japanese lives.
So, my book-end friends,
don't be on the shelf yourself,
take one finger, one thumb
- it's easily done -
be a book opener!

Silence, Please!

THE CIRCUS

Ladies and Gentlemen,
      Ponies! Ponies! Ponies!
      Here come the world-famous Camargue ponies!
            Gallop-a-gallop-a-gallop!
            Round and round and round they go.
            Gallop-a-gallop-a-gallop!
            Camargue ponies white as snow.

And now—
      The tiniest people in the world.
      Introducing the dwarf Minusculians.
            Low, lower, lowest,
            Down, down underneath—
            The smallest, dwarfest people
            who only reach your knees.

How are your nerves, my friends?
      Presenting the Libyan lions.
      The most roaring, rugged, rough and rummaging
      lions yet.
            Watch as they creep, crawl,
            stalk, spring, leap through
                  the flaming hoops
                  of gasoline—
                        Hop-là!

What would a circus be
      Without elephants?
      Those hulky, bulky,
            rumbling bumbling,
            trunk swinging, tail-stringing
                  pachyderms?
      A round of applause for—
                  the Elephants?

And now as the finale
      To wind up the show,
            The two Blondinis,
            Belle and her brother Beau.
                  High, touching the tent top
                  where we can only just see—
                  The high-wire balancing act
                  Of Belle and Beau Blondini!

Ego

I'm glad I'm me.
I wouldn't like to be
    a bear in hunting season,
    a cat that's up a tree
    with a bulldog underneath,
        a fly stuck in a window
    with a swat thats lifted up
    ready to be swatted –
        I'm glad I'm me.

I'm glad I'm me.
I wouldn't like to be
    a record with a scratch,
    a parrot in a cage,
    a football in a muddy match,
    a lion with a raging tooth –
    ache… or the dentist!
        I'm glad I'm me.

I'm glad I'm me.
I wouldn't like to be
a swimmer when there's sharks,
a student with no marks,
a car without an engine,
a train without a station,
a book without a cover,
one ski without the other,
a cat without a saucer,
a lawn without a mower,
a sister and no brother,
a dog without a bone,
a kitten without a home,
a schoolroom in the summer,
a race without a runner,
a hotdog and no bun —
Not one of these is fun.
They all have something wrong.
I'm glad I'm me, glad I'm me,
I'm me, I'm me, ME!

Skipping Rhyme 1

Hot-dogs
Hamburgers
Marshmallows
Chicken

Skipping Rhyme 2

Brownies
The Colonel's
MacDonald's
Home

Skipping Rhyme 3

Tongs
Forks
Chopsticks
Fingers

Skipping Rhyme 4

Pigs
Princes
Piranhas
Pixies

Name Calling

BANFF-a pan of porridge
set down by an angry chef

oe Canoe Canoe Canoe Canoe Canoe Canoe Can

   Nis-Nis-Nis-Nis
    Kan-Kan-Kan-Kan
     Lith-Lith-Lith-Lith
    NISKANLITH

       SHUSWAP...
      your "Nikes"
      for my "North Stars"

SOOKE-a sulky sailor

         The population of
          SPUZZUM
           is a dozen

BARRIERE, QUESNEL,
LACS DU BOIS, LE JEUNE, TRANQUILLE...
          BRITISH COLUMBIA!?

Nay Norbring Nell
  Tellelly
Nay Norbring Nell
Kan Konje Kan
  Keyerry
Kan Konje Kan
Voh Vorbring Fan
  Fanestre
Voh Vorbring Fan
Dees Pairing Vries
Vanjettes Miess
Dajahild Bries
Gahbrerry
Oh! Gahbrerry

THE MOUNTAIN

I'm climbing up the mountain,
     the mountain, the mountain.
I'm climbing up the mountain —
     I'm climbing with my eyes.

          then: eyelashes
                  nose
                  hands
                  elbows

I'm climbing up the mountain,
     the mountain, the mountain.
I'm climbing up the mountain —
     I'm never going to stop.
And when I reach the summit,
     the summit, the summit,
And when I reach the summit

     I'll sit upon the top.

Alphapoetics

Apple with six trees inside.

Bumblebees mean trouble for somebody's body.

Canary caged... shame yellow.

Doors can't close or open: they're helpless, swinging things.

Elves skip – their shoes are made for it!

F – effervescent "Eff".

Giants groan on and on...

Haughty, hi-falutin aitch.

Ink, switching on the white.

Jelly. Forget the Richter scale!

Kaleidoscope: clashing / colliding / fractured pattern.

Love... there's nothing to say...

Mermaids make men murmur.

Nobody likes nobody.

O – so perfect it's square.

Pockets – miniature museum for boys' artifacts

Questions Questions Questions

Rhubarb pie in long pie plates?

Shoelaces cooperate till that sudden, final, nervous breakdown.

Trout without sun or rain make rainbows.

Umbrellas – Up, I like their proud ribs, their tight-stretched skin.

V-a poor way to describe geese flight.

Waves waver then hurry and fall over themselves.

X – Don't be X; give us a X!

Yawl: lazy, poor relation of the hot-shot yacht.

Zoo – the animals' pen.